This Book Donated By

©Highsmith Inc. 1998

We Gather Together

CELEBRATING THE HARVEST SEASON

BY Wendy Pfeffer

ILLUSTRATED BY Linda Bleck

DUTTON CHILDREN'S BOOKS

DUTTON CHILDREN'S BOOKS
A division of Penguin Young Readers Group
Published by the Penguin Group
Penguin Group (USA) Inc., 375 Hudson Street, New York, New York 10014, U.S.A.
Penguin Group (Canada), 90 Eglinton Avenue East, Suite 700, Toronto, Ontario, Canada M4P 2Y3 (a division of Pearson
Penguin Canada Inc.) · Penguin Books Ltd, 80 Strand, London WC2R 0RL, England · Penguin Ireland, 25 St Stephen's
Green, Dublin 2, Ireland (a division of Penguin Books Ltd) · Penguin Group (Australia), 250 Camberwell Road,
Camberwell, Victoria 3124, Australia (a division of Pearson Australia Group Pty Ltd) · Penguin Books India Pvt Ltd, 11
Community Centre, Panchsheel Park, New Delhi - 110 017, India · Penguin Group (NZ), Cnr Airborne and Rosedale Roads,
Albany, Auckland 1310, New Zealand (a division of Pearson New Zealand Ltd) · Penguin Books (South Africa) (Pty) Ltd,
24 Sturdee Avenue, Rosebank, Johannesburg 2196, South Africa
Penguin Books Ltd, Registered Offices: 80 Strand, London WC2R 0RL, England

Library of Congress Cataloging-in-Publication Data

Pfeffer, Wendy, date.
We gather together : celebrating the harvest season / by Wendy Pfeffer; illustrated by Linda Bleck.
p. cm.
Includes bibliographical references.
ISBN 0-525-47669-5 (alk. paper)
1. Autumn—Juvenile literature. 2. Autumn—Study and teaching (Elementary)—Activity programs. 3. Autumnal
equinox—Juvenile literature. 4. Harvesting time—Juvenile literature. 5. Harvest festivals—Juvenile literature.
I. Bleck, Linda, ill. II. Title.
QB637.7.P44   2006
508.2—dc22   2006004340

Published in the United States by Dutton Children's Books,
a division of Penguin Young Readers Group
345 Hudson Street, New York, New York 10014
www.penguin.com/youngreaders

Designed by Irene Vandervoort

Manufactured in China   First Edition

1 3 5 7 9 10 8 6 4 2

For my family,

who gathers together many times each year.

How lucky we are!

W.P.

For my children, David and Sarah Mai

L.B.

During early autumn in the northern part of the earth,

    chipmunks pack their cheeks full of seeds

    to store in underground burrows.

Red fox pups hunt for rodents and fruit to eat,

    then bury leftovers to dig up when food is scarce.

Beavers store twigs and sticks underwater

    to chew when ice covers their pond.

As the sun appears lower in the southern sky each day,

the sun rises later each morning

and sets earlier each evening.

Days grow shorter, the nights cooler,

and the growing season ends.

Time to prepare for winter.

Black bears gobble honey, grubs, fruits, and roots,

building layers of fat for the cold days ahead.

People pick purple grapes, yellow squash,
orange pumpkins, and crisp red apples.
They husk corn, gather nuts, rake cranberries,
and enjoy the harvest season.

But today, there's little need for them
to stockpile food for winter as the animals do.
Ships, trucks, and cargo planes transport it
from parts of the world where fruits and
vegetables are still growing.
When it's winter in the Northern Hemisphere,
food is brought in from the Southern Hemisphere,
where it's summer.

FALL (autumnal) EQUINOX
DAY AND NIGHT EQUAL

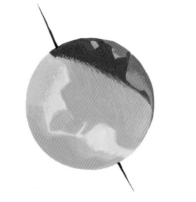

FALL
nights longer than days

days getting shorter

time to harvest

SUMMER
days longer than nights

days getting shorter

crops grow

WINTER SOLSTICE
THE SHORTEST DAY
WITH THE LEAST SUNSHINE

SUMMER SOLSTICE
THE LONGEST DAY
WITH THE MOST SUNSHINE

WINTER
nights longer than days

days getting longer

spring is coming

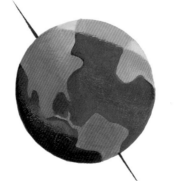

SPRING
days longer than nights

days getting longer

seedlings sprout

SPRING (vernal) EQUINOX
DAY AND NIGHT EQUAL

Different seasons are caused by the tilt of the earth
as it moves around the sun.
When the northern part of the earth tilts
toward the sun, the north gets lots of sunshine,
and it's summer there.
When the northern part of the earth tilts
away from the sun, the north gets less sunshine,
and it's winter.

Between summer and winter, around September 21,
the sun crosses the equator and shines
equally on both the northern and southern
parts of the earth.
On that day, in the northern part of the world,
summer ends and *autumn* begins.
Day and night have *equal* hours all over the world.
For many, the *autumnal equinox* signals a time
to harvest crops.

Each crop has its own growing season.

Most seedlings sprout with the cool spring rain

and thrive under the warm summer sun.

Sunshine helps a plant's leaves make the food

that is necessary for the plant to grow.

When autumn arrives, days are cooler.

Plants can no longer make the food they need,
and the growing season ends.

Time to gather in the crops.

Fruits and vegetables that ripen by autumn
must be harvested before winter's freezing
weather destroys them.

Three hundred thousand years ago,
    no one knew how to plant seeds
    to produce a bountiful harvest.
Cave dwellers picked berries,
    collected nuts, dug roots,
    and gathered wild plants.

Winters were hard for them.
They had to live on what they gathered
    and stored in the fall.

About ten thousand years ago,

  where Syria and Turkey are today,

  tribes learned to grow wheat and barley from seeds.

How exciting it must have been to plant one seed

  and produce a stalk with many!

Eight thousand years ago, in Egypt,

people discovered the warm climate

was perfect for farming.

The Nile River provided water,

and once each year its floodwaters

deposited rich, black, fertile soil on both sides.

Plants grew in abundance.

Gradually, farming spread to Asia.

About five thousand years ago, people grew food

   in a crescent-shaped area, where Iraq is now.

The Tigris River and small streams that fed it turned valleys

   into a Fertile Crescent of rich farmlands.

Each autumn in many lands, men, women, and children
worked all day, and even at night under the light
of a bright harvest moon.
They cut rice, threshed wheat, and gathered
bundles of barley.
A good harvest meant plenty of food to eat in the fall
and more to store for days when food was scarce.
Time to rejoice and have fun after hard, back-breaking work!

Over the centuries, people celebrated plentiful harvests
and passed down traditions, at different times,
in different places, and in different ways.
All over the world, harvest celebrations from the past
are still being carried on today.

Jewish families have gathered together at harvest time
for over three thousand years to celebrate Sukkot.

During this eight-day festival of thanksgiving,
they wave palm, myrtle, and willow branches,
then point them in all directions
to show that God is everywhere.

Some Jews build a hut, called a sukkah,
like the ones farmers once stayed in
to be near their crops during a busy harvest.
They decorate the huts with fruits and vegetables,
then invite friends and family to share
food and friendship.

People in southern India have celebrated Pongal,
a four-day rice festival, for over two thousand years.
On the first day, they decorate their front doors
with rice-flour designs and give thanks to the rain gods.
On the second day, they cook pongal, a sweet rice pudding,
and offer some to the sun god.

On the third day, they honor their cattle
to thank them for pulling the plows.
The fourth day, families and friends gather
on riverbanks to dance and enjoy a bountiful feast—
including, of course, freshly harvested rice.

The people of Japan have held rice festivals

for about two thousand years.

In spring, girls dressed in kimonos plant rice

while musicians play bells, drums, and flutes.

In summer, they hold a Lantern Festival

to express their joy as the rice ripens.

When fall comes, they celebrate the rice harvest

with parades and a dragon dance.

During their Moon Viewing ceremony, people sing

while watching shadows on the full moon.

Many think the shadows show a rabbit

making rice cakes.

For over seven hundred years, Nigerians have held a fall festival
to give thanks for yams, the first crop harvested.
On the night before the festivities begin,
the old, wrinkled yams are thrown out.

The next day, new yams are offered to the gods and ancestors,

in appreciation of a successful harvest.

Dancers wear raffia skirts and masks that portray turtles, lizards, trees,

and the sun or moon to celebrate a cycle of nature.

Hundreds of years ago, the English believed

    that the spirit of their wheat lived

    in the last bundle they cut.

In each field they twisted it into the shape of a doll.

Since they called wheat "corn,"

    these dolls were named "corn dollies."

They were hung in barns or churches during the winter,

then plowed back into the earth in the spring

to insure a good harvest in autumn.

People still make "corn dollies," just for fun.

Pilgrims from England arrived in America
     in the fall of 1620, too late to plant crops.
That winter, many died from hunger and sickness.
When spring came, the surviving Pilgrims
     sowed wheat seeds.
A Native American tribe, the Wampanoags,
     showed them how to plant maize, or corn.

The following autumn, the harvest was fruitful.
The Pilgrims planned a celebration to share this blessing.
Wampanoag men hunted and killed five deer
     to bring to the feast.

The Pilgrims stayed busy, too.

Men brought ducks, geese, turkeys, fish, and oysters.

Women prepared corn bread and cranberries while children turned meat on spits over an open fire.

Games and feasting lasted three days.

Bountiful harvests have been celebrated since earliest times.

People all over the world still celebrate a fruitful year of farming
with fun, feasts, and festivals.

They enjoy corn, rice, yams, apples, pumpkins, cranberries,
and other fruits and vegetables of the harvest season.

Autumn, with its brilliant colors and delicious gifts of nature,
offers friends and families a time to gather together
and give thanks for all their blessings.

EQUINOX FACTS

An equinox occurs when the center of the sun appears directly over the equator and shines equally on both the northern and southern parts of the earth. Day and night are equal all over the world.

Equinox means "equal night." On that day, everywhere on earth, there are twelve hours of light and twelve hours of dark.

There are four seasons in each year. A day called the *vernal equinox* welcomes the first day of spring. The *summer solstice*, the longest day of the year, tells us summer has arrived. The *autumnal equinox* greets autumn. And winter begins on the *winter solstice*, the shortest day. We enjoy four seasons because the earth tilts.

Around March 21, the spring equinox, the sun appears to cross the equator as it moves from south to north. Day and night are equal all over the world. It's the first day of spring, time to plant our seeds.

Around June 21, the summer solstice, the northern part of the world receives the direct rays of the sun. We have the longest day of the year, the first day of summer, when our plants grow.

Around September 21, the autumnal equinox, the sun appears to cross the equator again as it moves from north to south. Day and night are equal all over the world. It's the first day of autumn, time to start harvesting crops.

The full moon nearest to the first day of autumn, or the autumnal equinox, is called the harvest moon. Its bright light allowed people to harvest crops late in the night.

After the autumnal equinox, the northern part of the world receives only the indirect rays of the sun. The days get shorter and the nights longer until the winter solstice, around December 21. Then the cycle begins again.

PROVE THE SUN RISES DUE EAST ON BOTH EQUINOXES

What you need:

- *paper and pencil*
- *a compass*

What to do between September 15 and 20:

1. Choose a time in the morning, such as when you're waiting for the school bus.

2. Choose a spot where you can sit and draw for a few minutes.

3. Check your compass and face east.

4. Sketch what you see around you: houses, trees, telephone poles—but not the sun.

5. Write *north* on the top left side of your paper. Write *east* on the top middle. Write *south* on the top right side.

6. Make seven copies of your sketch on a copier machine. (See art above.)

What to do around the 21st of September, October, November, December, January, February, and March:

1. Check your calendar. In September and March, go out on the exact equinox days.

2. At the same time of day that you made your original sketch, go to your chosen spot with a pencil, compass, and one copy of the sketch.

3. Check your compass and face east.

4. Sketch the position of the sun. (In September, you should be facing the sun. In December, the sun should be slightly to your right. In March, you should be facing the sun.)

5. Write the date and time on each sketch.

6. After March, put your sketches in order, from September to March.

7. Do your sketches show the sun rising in due east in both September and March?

On both the autumnal equinox and the vernal equinox, the sun rises due east and sets due west. You could also do this experiment in the evening by facing west instead of east. Follow the directions above, but change east to west and reverse north and south.

SHOW HOW THE TILT OF THE EARTH MAKES THE SEASONS

Long ago, people thought that the closer the sun is to the earth, the warmer that part of the world would be. That's not true. Actually, the northern part of the world is closer to the sun in January, when it's winter. It's farther away in July, when it's summer. The earth's tilt makes the seasons, not its distance from the sun. The tilt of the earth causes the sun's rays to hit it at different angles. The angle at which the sun shines on a certain place determines whether it is warm or cool there. Here's how you can prove it.

What you need:

- *a flashlight*
- *a piece of dark paper*
- *a globe*

What you will prove:

1. When the sun is directly overhead in summer, its rays are strong and the temperature is warm.

2. When the sun is low in the sky in winter, its rays are weak and the temperature is cool.

What to do:

1. Shine the flashlight straight down on the dark paper.

2. See how strong the light shines on that small round area.

3. Tilt the flashlight the same distance from the paper as it was in Step 1.

4. See how the light is spread out over a greater oblong area.

5. Now hold the flashlight straight and shine it on the northern part of the globe.

6. See how strong the light shines on a small round area. When the sun appears overhead in the sky, its rays shine straight down, hitting a small area. The light and heat are concentrated there, and it's summer.

7. Tilt the flashlight and shine it on the northern part of the globe.

8. See how the light is spread out over a large oblong area of the globe.

9. When the sun appears low in the sky, its heat and light are diluted and weak over a large area. Less heat and light reach each place there, and it's winter.

MAKE "EQUINOX" CORN MUFFINS TO SHARE

The Wampanoags taught the Pilgrims to dry corn, mix it with boiling water, and bake it into thin cakes. Hunters and traders took these cakes with them when they traveled. The name "Journey cakes" was later changed to "Johnny cakes." Since then, many recipes for corn bread, muffins, and cakes have been written down. Here's one for corn muffins.

What you need:

2 cups cornmeal
1 teaspoon baking soda
1 teaspoon salt
2 eggs

2 cups buttermilk
chocolate icing (for night)
vanilla icing (optional, for day)

mixing bowl, large spoon, teaspoon, measuring cup, and a 12-muffin nonstick pan

What to do:

1. Ask an adult to help you. Turn the oven on to 450 degrees.
2. Mix the cornmeal, baking soda, and salt in the bowl.
3. Add the eggs and buttermilk and beat until blended.
4. Spoon into the muffin cups.
5. Bake at 450 degrees for 10 to 15 minutes.
6. Cool thoroughly.
7. Ice half of each muffin with chocolate icing for night.
8. Ice the other half with vanilla icing for daytime,
   OR leave half yellow for daylight.

Make twice as many as you need so you can share half of what you bake with others, AND/OR cut the muffins in two equal parts and share half. What else can you share half? An apple? a sandwich? a cookie?

Talk about how every muffin represents the equinox, when each 24 hours is divided into two equal times. Day is 12 hours long. Night is 12 hours long.
ENJOY!

MAKE NIGERIAN HARVEST MASKS AND CELEBRATE

Masks have often been designed and worn to celebrate a cycle of nature. One cycle is planting seeds, caring for seedlings, and harvesting ripe fruits and vegetables.

What you need:
- *9 x 12 paper*
- *9 x 12 cardboard or oak tag*
- *a pencil*
- *scissors*
- *string*

What to do:

1. Plan a design on paper. Use animals, trees, the sun, moon, or your own ideas of a harvest celebration. Turtles can be drawn with the shell divided into twelve parts, one for each month of the year. Your design may tell a story.

2. Cut the cardboard or oak tag the shape and size of your face.

3. Draw and color your design on the cardboard.

4. Make two small holes for your eyes to see through.

5. Punch out a small hole on each side.

6. Put the string through the holes on each side.

7. To put on your mask, tie the string around your head.

8. Celebrate with music, dance, songs, and your artwork.

WRITE ABOUT OTHER HARVEST FESTIVALS

Here are some other harvest festivals you can research and write about:

China's Moon Festival

Incas' Corn Harvest Celebration

Ancient Egyptian Harvest Parade

Ancient Greek Harvest Festival

Hopi Corn Dance

Iroquois Green Corn Dance

Germany's Oktoberfest

Cherokee Harvest Festival

Czech Republic Harvest Celebration

Barbados Sugar Cane Festival

Japan's Labor Thanksgiving Day

Find other harvest celebrations held throughout the world to write about.

FURTHER READING

Henes, Donna. *Celestially Auspicious Occasions: Seasons, Cycles & Celebrations.*
New York: Perigee: Putnam/Penguin, 1996.

Jackson, Ellen B. *The Autumn Equinox: Celebrating the Harvest.* Brookfield, CT:
Millbrook Press, 2000.

Kalman, Bobbie. *We Celebrate the Harvest.* New York: Crabtree Publishing Co., 1986.

Markle, Sandra. *Exploring Autumn.* New York: Atheneum, 1991.

Rosen, Mike. *Autumn Festivals.* New York: The Bookwright Press, 1990.

Russell, Ching Yeung. *Moon Festival.* Honesdale, PA: Boyds Mills Press, 1997.

Tresselt, Alvin. *Autumn Harvest.* New York: Lothrop, Lee & Shepherd, 1951.

WEB SITES

http://www.glyphweb.com/esky/concepts/autumnalequinox.html
See an informative diagram of the earth revolving around the sun and learn
the exact times that equinoxes will occur each year up to 2010.

http://www.equinox-and-solstice.com
Learn more about the vernal equinox, summer solstice, autumnal equinox,
and winter solstice.

http://www.my-ecoach.com/online/webresourcelist.php?rlid=793
Explore numerous sites on harvest and autumnal celebrations. Check a listing
of harvest festivals from *A* (African) to *Z* (Zambian).